Practical

Disciple

A Bible Study Based on the
New Testament Book of James
by
Robert L. Tasler

NOTICE OF RIGHTS

AUTHOR'S NOTE

The Bible references used in this work are from the English Standard Version, 2011 edition, an updating of the Revised Standard Version of 1971, published by Crossway Bibles. Thanks to my dear wife for her proofing-reading.

ALSO BY THE AUTHOR
(Paperback and E-Book)

Daily Walk With Jesus
Daily Word From Jesus
Spreading The Word
Reflections
Murder At Palm Park
Matrimony At Palm Park
Miracle at Palm Park
Bobby Was A Farmer Boy

(E-Book only)

Country Preacher
Small Town Preacher
Immigrant Son

(Bible Study)
The Hopeful Disciple
The Practical Disciple

Table of Contents

Preface to the Letter of James

I personally view the Letter of James as the most practical book in the New Testament. The author deals with such topics as temptation, good deeds, listening, favoritism, keeping one's tongue in check, worldliness, boasting, greed, wealth and patience.

While James is short on theological depth, its practical approach to everyday problems is helpful. James does not display the humility and hopefulness of Simon Peter. Rather, he sticks to the basics of what a Christian man, woman or child should and should not do in their speech and dealings with others.

Martin Luther thought James spoke too little of faith and too much of works, and at one time labeled this book, *"an epistle of straw."* He said it had usefulness but lacked the power and depth of Paul's writings, so he said, *"I cannot include James among the Bible's chief books, but there are still many good sayings there for a Christian to learn."*

Although Luther's early attitude towards James was shaped by his concern that the Roman Church had overshadowed the Gospel with works of the Law, he came to value the instructions and teaching James had for Christians. Luther came to view this book differently with time. His concern for Gospel is clarified in the 62th of his 95 Theses: *"The true treasure of the Church is the most holy Gospel of the glory and grace of God."*

James speaks simply and directly to concerns they have in their daily lives. For this reason alone, James is useful to study in modern times.

While I encourage the use of several Bible versions, in this study I have used the English Standard Version throughout for the purpose of having the same words before us. The Practical Disciple can be used for either group or individual Bible study. God bless all who read the Letter of James and this short book which helps to clarify the message of James.

+ Rev. Robert L. Tasler, 2014 +

Dedication

To my lifelong friend, Rev. Harley Johnson, for his dedicated service in the Kingdom. We played together as farm kids, became pastors in the same Lutheran denomination and remained close friends through the years. In 2015, Harley went to be with the Lord.

"The Practical Disciple"

A Study of the Letter of St. James

Session 1
Overview of the Letter of James
+ + +

AUTHOR

The James identified as author in 1:1 is most certainly the half-brother of Jesus and leader of the Jerusalem Council (Acts 15). Four men have this name in the New Testament. The author could not have been John's brother James, as he had already died in 44 AD, too early for the writing of this letter. The other two men named James did not have the influence or stature that this writer had.

James was one of several siblings Jesus had through Mary and her husband Joseph. James was perhaps the oldest, since he heads the list noted in Matthew 13:55. He did not at first believe in Jesus and even challenged Him and His mission as noted in John 7:2-5.

How do these passages mention James?

1 Corinthians 15:7_____

Galatians 2:9_____

Galatians 1:19_____

Acts 21:18_____

Acts 12:17_____

Acts 15:13_____

Jude 1:1_____

1

DATE

While some scholars date the writing of James in the early 60's, it may have been written even before 50 AD, making it one of the earliest of the New Testament books. Four reasons can be given for this early dating.

1. The letter's Jewish nature suggests it was written while the church was predominantly Jewish.

2. The letter has a simple church order. Church officers are called "Elders" (5:14) and "teachers" (3:1). "Elders" in Paul's later letters were pastors.

3. There's no mention of the "Gentile circumcision" controversy which the Jerusalem Council debated in 50 AD.

4. Synagogues in this letter are the designated meeting places (2:2) and this practice quickly disappeared in the early church.

   a. What is the relationship between the Pastor and the Elders in your congregation?

   _____

   b. What was the Gentile Circumcision controversy?

   _____

   c. If not synagogues, where do you think early Christians met?

   _____

RECIPIENTS

James 1:1 identifies the recipients of this letter as *"the twelve tribes scattered among the nations."* While this phrase could apply to all Christians, it could also apply to Christians with Jewish origins. A Jewish audience might also explain the Jewish nature of the letter.

d. What words in James 5:4 show this?

_____

e. What does 2:1 tell us for certain about the letter?

_____

f. What happened in Acts 8:1? How might this explain the Jewish "dispersion?"

_____

PLACE

Since the letter assumes its readers are very familiar with Jewish tradition, this detail may point to the place of writing as being in Jerusalem or another place in Israel. The general material of this letter, however, makes the place of writing less important than with some of the other New Testament writings.

LUTHER ON JAMES

"The author wanted to guard against those who relied on faith without works. He tries to accomplish this by harping on the law what the apostle [Paul] accomplished by urging people to love. I do not include James among the chief New Testament books, though I would not prevent anyone from reading it."

5. What one main aspect about the letter of James do you think made Luther dislike it, or at least not count in as important as other letters?

_____

3

6. Does Luther's opinion of a Bible book affect how you understand or accept it? Why?

_____

7. What influence does Martin Luther still have on the Church today?

_____

THEME

James writes on the various topics in his letter in a random manner. It is almost as if he started his letter and let the Holy Spirit move him from one topic to the next, addressing the problems he saw among Christians. What topics are brought up in these verses?

1. 1:2-3 _____

1:19-20 _____

2:1-3 _____

2:14-16 _____

3:1-3 _____

4:1-4 _____

5:1-3 _____

5:7-8 _____

5:13-15 _____

5:19-20 _____

The letter stops abruptly with Verse 20, as if he was interrupted and didn't finish, or even if the last part of his letter was lost. Whatever the case, the letter ends without the usual final greetings or benediction.

Another interesting note: The letter of James makes little reference to the passion, death or resurrection of Jesus. He speaks of the Christ several times, yet teaches us little about Him. One would think James would follow up with a witness for Jesus, but James simply stays with his theme of what it means to live a Christian life. His purpose deals with behavior more than theology.

It is an overlooked fact that while Jesus had no close relatives among his disciples, two of His half brothers, James and Jude, wrote epistles that are included in the books of the New Testament.

As you study the letter of James, pray for wisdom and the will to do what you know is right. Look also for practical solutions to the issues that challenge your personal life or congregation. The letter of James will give you good advice.

God's people are still sinners and will make mistakes. They will hurt each other and need to confess their faults and forgive each other. When troubles arise in church or family, rely on the love of God the Father, and rejoice in His wonderful gifts of salvation through eternal life. These gifts can never be taken away.

+ + +

Heavenly Father, thank You for this letter from James, inspired by Your Holy Spirit. Amen

One thing I learned from this session:

"The Practical Disciple"

A Study of the Letter of St. James

Session 2
The Letter of James 1:1-18

+ + +

Greeting

1 *¹ James, a servant of God and of the Lord Jesus Christ, To the twelve tribes in the Dispersion: Greetings. ² Count it all joy, my brothers, when you meet trials of various kinds, ³ for you know that the testing of your faith produces steadfastness. ⁴ And let steadfastness have its full effect, that you may be perfect and complete, lacking in nothing. ⁵ If any of you lacks wisdom, let him ask God, who gives generously to all without reproach, and it will be given him. ⁶ But let him ask in faith, with no doubting, for the one who doubts is like a wave of the sea that is driven and tossed by the wind. ⁷ For that person must not suppose that he will receive anything from the Lord; ⁸ he is a double-minded man, unstable in all his ways. ⁹ Let the lowly brother boast in his exaltation, ¹⁰ and the rich in his humiliation, because like a flower of the grass he will pass away. ¹¹ For the sun rises with its scorching heat and withers the grass; its flower falls, and its beauty perishes. So also will the rich man fade away in the midst of his pursuits. ¹² Blessed is the man who remains steadfast under trial, for when he has stood the test he will receive the crown of life, which God has promised to those who love him. ¹³ Let no one say when he is tempted, "I am being tempted by God," for God cannot be tempted with evil, and he himself tempts no one.*

^{14} *But each person is tempted when he is lured and enticed by his own desire.* ^{15} *Then desire when it has conceived gives birth to sin, and sin when it is fully grown brings forth death.* ^{16} *Do not be deceived, my beloved brothers.* ^{17} *Every good gift and every perfect gift is from above, coming down from the Father of lights with whom there is no variation or shadow due to change.* ^{18} *Of his own will he brought us forth by the word of truth, that we should be a kind of first fruits of his creatures.*

+ + +

James and Jude were biological half-brothers of Jesus, although some traditions state they were cousins or sons of Joseph from a former marriage. There appears to be some family jealousy of Jesus' ministry as noted in Mark 3:21.

1. What do we read of this in John 7:5, 12?

_____

2. According to St. Paul in 1 Corinthians 15:7, what was James privileged to be?

_____

3. In verse 2, James speaks of various kinds of trials. How might his struggle to understand Jesus' ministry relate to "trials"?

_____

8

4. What does James says that testing produces?

_____

5. How can steadfastness make us complete? What do you think James means here?

_____

6. In verse 5, for what does James say we should ask God?

_____

7. How should we pray for this, according to verse 6?

_____

8. James pictures a "doubter" as a wave on a lake that comes and goes, here and there with no purpose, stability or direction. What doubts have you struggled with?

_____

9. In verse 7-8, James seems to be saying a doubter is an unfit person, unstable and unworthy of God's blessings. Do you agree or disagree with this? Why?

_____

10. In verses 9-10, a poor person is contrasted with a rich one. Wealth often brings privileges that look like self-accomplishment. Give a reason or two why James warns the rich not to "pat themselves on the back" according to verse 11?

_____

_____

11. How is verse 12 linked with verse 2?

_____

12. What do you think is meant by "the crown of life"?

_____

13. Verse 13 jumps to the subject of temptation. James seems to be writing his letter by association, with one subject leading into another. How do people write letters to each other today?

_____

14. How does James 1:13 compare with Matthew 6:13?

_____

15. What is the source of temptation according to verse 14?

_____

16. In verse 15, what does James say gives birth to sin?

_____

17. Verse 16 states people can be deceived by the world, but not by God. What does verse 17 tell that God provides us?

_____

18. Why would James refer to God as the "Father of lights"?

_____

19. Compare James 1:17b with Hebrews 13:8.

_____

20. Verse 18 says God the Father created us. In what manner does it say He did this?

_____

21. What does verse 18 say is the purpose of God's creating us?

_____

+ + +

Heavenly Father, when our faith is tested help us to remain faithful to Jesus. Amen

11

One thing I learned from this session:

"The Practical Disciple"
A Study of the Letter of St. James

Session 3
The Letter of James 1:19-27
+ + +

Hearing and Doing the Word

1 *19 Know this, my beloved brothers: let every person be quick to hear, slow to speak, slow to anger; 20 for the anger of man does not produce the righteousness of God. 21 Therefore put away all filthiness and rampant wickedness and receive with meekness the implanted word, which is able to save your souls. 22 But be doers of the word, and not hearers only, deceiving yourselves. 23 For if anyone is a hearer of the word and not a doer, he is like a man who looks intently at his natural face in a mirror. 24 For he looks at himself and goes away and at once forgets what he was like. 25 But the one who looks into the perfect law, the law of liberty, and perseveres, being no hearer who forgets but a doer who acts, he will be blessed in his doing. 26 If anyone thinks he is religious and does not bridle his tongue but deceives his heart, this person's religion is worthless. 27 Religion that is pure and undefiled before God, the Father, is this: to visit orphans and widows in their affliction, and to keep oneself unstained from the world.*

+ + +

James now switches to the need of showing one's faith and what a person does. He begins his comments with a person's speech.

What a Christian person says reflects directly on that person's faith. In a day such as ours, the notion of "free speech" has led western people, including Christians, to believe they can say whatever they want, wherever they want, regardless of how vulgar or hurtful it may be.

James would surely be appalled at what he would hear in conversation or over the public airwaves. His practical words in this section will speak to how a Christian should or should not speak, whether publicly or privately.

1. What do you think James' use of "beloved brothers" in verse 19 probably means? Who were the majority of his readers?

_____

2. What three things does James urge of Christians in verse 19?

    a. _____

    b. _____

    c. _____

3. James has urged three behaviors but embellishes one, anger. Is anger a sin? Why or why not?

_____

4. What does verse 20 say anger can produce?

_____

5. Why is anger such a dangerous emotion?

_____

6. Can you think of any world situation in which anger seems to play a large role?

_____

7. To what does the phrase, "righteousness of God," refer? God's nature or our behavior? Why?

_____

8. Verse 21 speaks of abstaining from the sinfulness of the world. What do you think causes such *"filthiness and rampant wickedness"* in our world today?

_____

9. Would James have considered our world worse than his world?

_____

10. "Receive with meekness the implanted word" has two important phrases. How do these words relate to Christianity?

    a. Receive_____

    b. Implanted_____

15

11. What, according to verse 21, is the source of our salvation?

_____

12. What is the difference between a "doer" and a "hearer" in verse 22?

_____

13. Which is easier to be? Why?

_____

14. What does "doing the Word" mean?

_____

15. What should "hearing the Word" lead us to do?

_____

16. In verse 23, James uses a mirror, both as a way to see our sins, and also to reflect God's righteousness. Our "natural face" is our sin, something we can quickly forget (verse 24). Why is our sin so easy to forget?

_____

17. In light of this, how could guilt become a useful thing?

_____

16

18. Verse 25 has an important concept. What do you think James means by looking into the "perfect law"?

_____

19. How does that person "persevere"?

_____

20. In verse 26, James' use of "religious" and "religion" show that religion is not only a set of beliefs, but the deeds a person does because of one's beliefs. In this verse, what shows whether or not that person's "religion" is valid or true?

_____

21. Can you think of ways that a Christian today can "deceive" himself into believing he's doing the right thing, but is not?

_____

22. Verse 27 is important to James' entire letter, for it lays out his central precept: Genuine righteousness seeks to serve others. By what two actions does James say a Christian can show this?

a._____

b._____

23. Why does it seem especially hard today to "keep oneself unstained from the world?"

_____

Heavenly Father, help us to live in this world as a witness to You, and not be "of this world". Amen

<u>One thing I learned from this session:</u>

"The Practical Disciple"
A Study of the Letter of St. James

Session 4
The Letter of James 2:1-13
+ + +

Show No Partiality

2 *¹ My brothers, show no partiality as you hold the faith in our Lord Jesus Christ, the Lord of glory. ² For if a man wearing a gold ring and fine clothing comes into your assembly, and a poor man in shabby clothing also comes in, ³ and if you pay attention to the one who wears the fine clothing and say, "You sit here in a good place," while you say to the poor man, "You stand over there," or, "Sit down at my feet," ⁴ have you not then made distinctions among yourselves and become judges with evil thoughts? ⁵ Listen, my beloved brothers, has not God chosen those who are poor in the world to be rich in faith and heirs of the kingdom, which he has promised to those who love him? ⁶ But you have dishonored the poor man. Are not the rich the ones who oppress you, and the ones who drag you into court? ⁷ Are they not the ones who blaspheme the honorable name by which you were called? ⁸ If you really fulfill the royal law according to the Scripture, "You shall love your neighbor as yourself," you are doing well. ⁹ But if you show partiality, you are committing sin and are convicted by the law as transgressors. ¹⁰ For whoever keeps the whole law but fails in one point has become accountable for all of it. ¹¹ For he who said, "Do not commit adultery," also said, "Do not murder." If you do not commit adultery but do murder, you have*

19

become a transgressor of the law. [12] So speak and so act as those who are to be judged under the law of liberty. [13] For judgment is without mercy to one who has shown no mercy. Mercy triumphs over judgment.

+ + +

James confronts an apparent problem in some of the churches. When a new "movement" begins, such as the early Christian church, there is joy and anticipation over what God is doing. There are also practical concerns to address such as theology, leadership and funding.

To grow and become strong, a congregation requires paying close attention to such concerns, as well as to bring in new members. Practical concerns may move some members to seek new members based on their wealth or skills.

If a church needs musical skills, the musician may be sought and preferred over the needy family. If teachers or leaders or builders are needed, we may pursue them and neglect others who come. It is not "partiality" to be grateful and anxious that certain members are brought in. God brings them, and we are glad they have come. But their skills or wealth must not become our primary reason for seeking them.

When members "wine and dine" the wealthy or influential, it can lead to resentment and factions. This is what James now confronts.

1. How do you treat the wealthy who come to your congregation?

2. Can you share a story of this happening in your congregation? What was the end result?

_____

3. Have you had experience with one or more poor families coming into your congregation? Did you help them? Was it a positive or negative experience?

_____

4. Have you been part of a congregation that needed to raise funds for a building project? How do you view the fund-raising practices you have experienced?

_____

5. Showing partiality is giving unfair judgment based on worldly criteria. What can this do in a congregation?

_____

6. Have you experienced the joy of taking in a poor family as members and they become a great blessing there? Care to relate your experience?

_____

7. James uses glaring comparisons (*"Take this good seat"* versus *"Sit in the corner"*). What are some subtle comparisons that can show we are being partial?

_____

8. In a time of the high cost of building, what are some practices a congregation might engage in that can help build up a congregation without seeking wealthy members?

_____

9. What do you think James is saying in verse 5?

_____

10. What is James implying about the wealthy in verse 6-7?

_____

11. Is James being "judgmental" or "partial" in his comments about the wealthy? What does "wealthy" mean to us today?

_____

12. In verse 8, James states that showing partiality breaks the second great commandment. What is it? (see Mark 12:31)

_____

13. Where have you heard verse 10 before? Can you find another Bible passage that states this?

_____

14. Is "murder" the same as "killing"? What's the difference?

_____

15. In verse 11, James equates all the commandments. He has already said, *"If you break one, you have broken them all"*. What does this mean for all people, including the faithful and loving Christian person?

_____

16. In verse 12, James speaks of *"the law of liberty"*. What do you think he means by this phrase?

_____

17. James is exhorting his readers to remember they were counted righteous for Christ's sake. How does Almighty God consider both the wealthy and the poor?

_____

18. Verse 13 has a powerful message. What do you think is meant by James' statement, *"judgment is without mercy to one who has shown no mercy"*.

_____

19. How do the words, *"Mercy triumphs over judgment"* compare with the words of Hosea 6:6?

_____

20. What message might James have for a congregation in the midst of a building program or other large funding effort?

_____

Judging others based on appearance, wealth, skills or status is inconsistent with righteous living. The desire for wealth leads us to lift up the wealthy and look down on the poor, but this is not God's way. He calls all people to faith in Christ and grants all the faithful the same gift of eternal life. He gives us all a new status that the world can never give. We are God's children!

Heavenly Father, help all congregations to be accepting and loving to all its members. Amen

One thing I learned from this session:

"The Practical Disciple"

A Study of the Letter of St. James

Session 5
The Letter of James 2:14-26

+ + +

Faith Without Works Is Dead

2 *¹⁴ What good is it, my brothers, if someone says he has faith but does not have works? Can that faith save him? ¹⁵ If a brother or sister is poorly clothed and lacking in daily food, ¹⁶ and one of you says to them, "Go in peace, be warmed and filled," without giving them the things needed for the body, what good is that? ¹⁷ So also faith by itself, if it does not have works, is dead.¹⁸ But someone will say, "You have faith and I have works." Show me your faith apart from your works, and I will show you my faith by my works. ¹⁹ You believe that God is one; you do well. Even the demons believe — and shudder! ²⁰ Do you want to be shown, you foolish person, that faith apart from works is useless? ²¹ Was not Abraham our father justified by works when he offered up his son Isaac on the altar? ²² You see that faith was active along with his works, and faith was completed by his works; ²³ and the Scripture was fulfilled that says, "Abraham believed God, and it was counted to him as righteousness" — and he was called a friend of God. ²⁴ You see that a person is justified by works and not by faith alone. ²⁵ And in the same way was not also Rahab the prostitute justified by works when she received the messengers and sent them out by another way? ²⁶ For as the body apart from the spirit is dead, so also faith apart from works is dead.*

+ + +

James makes the transition from showing partiality to how faith shows itself in one's life. This section was problematic with Martin Luther who was concerned some might interpret James as teaching justification by both faith and works, and not by faith alone.

Some scholars wrongly state this passage shows that Paul and James taught conflicting doctrines. James is addressing a misunderstanding about faith. His reasoning is not in conflict with Paul's teachings.

1. Verse 14 states, *"if someone says he has faith but does not have works"?* To this point in James, faith has been viewed positively. James now uses a definition of faith that separates faith from works. Do you think that is possible? Why?

_____

2. What kind of example does James give in verse 15?

_____

3. Why is the reaction, *"be warmed and filled"* insufficient?

_____

4. Is it possible for believers always to provide *"things needed for the body"* (verse 16)? What is James telling us here?

_____

5. Is not faith alone needed for justification? Why could verse 17 still be true?

_____

6. Read verse 18 carefully. What is the *"someone"* quoted there actually saying?

_____

7. James sets forth his basic premise in the last part of verse 18. What is it?

_____

8. In verse 19, what is implied by his use of "faith" here?

_____

9. What is the difference between "faith" and "belief?"

_____

10. What is the content of a demon's "belief"?

_____

11. What value does faith have if there are no good works with it?

_____

12. James now gives several well known Old Testament examples of people who showed their faith by their works. What good deeds did these persons do to show their faith?

   a. Abraham_____

   b. Rahab _____

13. Verse 22 is the main point in this section. "*You see that faith was active along with his works, and faith was completed by his works.*" Verse 24 could mistakenly be quoted by itself, *"You see that a person is justified by works and not by faith alone."* What will be the result if verse 24 is quoted without verse 22?

_____

14. In verse 23, what does James say Abraham was called? (This is not found in the Bible but in traditional Jewish literature.)

_____

15. Who is given this title in Exodus 33:11?_____

16. James uses two very different people in his examples of faith showing itself in deeds. Why is Rahab a questionable example?

_____

17. How is verse 26 a good summary of this section?

_____

18. Living the Christian life is not easy today. The world tempts us to be "partial Christians" but God calls us to total faith in Him. Believers today need to be aware of how easy it is to compromise their faith. Tell how compromising faith might be done in these situations:

a. *"My Sunday life has nothing to do with my business."*

_____

b. *"My work as a scientist is separate from my Christianity."*

_____

c. *"I look for the best return on my investments, not how they are made."*

_____

d. *"I judge TV and movies strictly by their entertainment value."*

_____

e. *"Religion and politics must be kept totally separate."*

_____

19. Are any of the above statements partially true? If so, how can a Christian follow them and still remain faithful to God?

_____

Only the Holy Spirit can enable us to live by trusting in God and His provision. The Spirit works through Word and Sacrament. This is why worship and Bible study are important in life.

O Holy Spirit, guide us to trust in our Lord Jesus by faith, and help our faith to show itself in good deeds to benefit others. Amen.

One thing I learned from this session:

"The Practical Disciple"

A Study of the Letter of St. James

Session 6
The Letter of James 3:1-12

+ + +

Taming the Tongue

3 ¹ *Not many of you should become teachers, my brothers, for you know that we who teach will be judged with greater strictness.* ² *For we all stumble in many ways. And if anyone does not stumble in what he says, he is a perfect man, able also to bridle his whole body.* ³ *If we put bits into the mouths of horses so that they obey us, we guide their whole bodies as well.* ⁴ *Look at the ships also: though they are so large and are driven by strong winds, they are guided by a very small rudder wherever the will of the pilot directs.* ⁵ *So also the tongue is a small member, yet it boasts of great things. How great a forest is set ablaze by such a small fire!* ⁶ *And the tongue is a fire, a world of unrighteousness. The tongue is set among our members, staining the whole body, setting on fire the entire course of life, and set on fire by hell.* ⁷ *For every kind of beast and bird, of reptile and sea creature, can be tamed and has been tamed by mankind,* ⁸ *but no human being can tame the tongue. It is a restless evil, full of deadly poison.* ⁹ *With it we bless our Lord and Father, and with it we curse people who are made in the likeness of God.* ¹⁰ *From the same mouth come blessing and cursing. My brothers, these things ought not to be so.* ¹¹ *Does a spring pour forth from the same opening both fresh and salt water?* ¹² *Can a fig tree, my brothers, bear olives, or a grapevine produce figs? Neither can a salt pond yield fresh water.*

+ + +

There are only two ways to live. Either we live by the "wisdom of the world" or we live by "wisdom from above." James warns against accepting the world's pattern of life which leads to selfishness, deception, greed or other evils. Christians who seek to follow God's wisdom still struggle with these sins, including the temptation to think of themselves as better than others.

The wisdom of God is totally different from the wisdom of the world. Almighty God has forgiven us in Jesus Christ and helps us resist the sinful actions and attitudes that tempt us. By the Spirit's power we now can "walk the walk" as well as "talk the talk."

1. James addresses our speech as Christians, and begins with a warning about striving to become a teacher. What is the reason for his warning?

_____

2. What does verse 2a tell us? How do we know this?

_____

3. What do you think James means in verse 2b?

_____

4. A horse's bridle can guide the whole horse. How can it do this?

_____

5. James' metaphor in verses 3-4 includes a ship's rudder. In both cases, what is he telling us about the Christian life?

_____

6. It seems today as if people care little about what they say, whether crude or offensive. This has resulted in laws being passed to curb free speech. What would James say about "free speech"?

_____

7. Is the tongue (verse 5a) the actual culprit in sins of speech? If not, what is?

_____

8. Verse 5b speaks of forest fires. What does it take to set a forest on fire? How does that compare with a tongue?

_____

9. In verse 6 James says the "world" is always opposed to God. How can words reflect sin in the world? (see Mark 7:14ff) How is the tongue set on fire by hell?

_____

10. Verse 7 shows that at the time of James, mankind had "subdued" nature and most of its animals. Which verses in Genesis 1 and 2 give us the command of God to do this?

_____

11. If we can tame the animals, why can't we tame the tongue? Can laws about speech help us do this?

_____

12. *"Sticks and stones may break my bones, but words can never hurt me."* Why is this statement not true?

_____

13. Verse 9 shows James' reasoning for condemning the untamed tongue.

With it we _____, yet still _____.

14. Verse 10 calls for consistency. Righteous people have received from God the *"implanted word"* (1:20-21), so our lives should reflect what God has made us to be. If we are not doing this, how can we change?

_____

15. Verses 11-12 reason that creation itself shows it cannot be two different things at once. Yet the human tongue goes against nature. Why?

_____

16. Jesus speaks of this in Matthew 7:15-19. How can a Christian deal with the evil use of speech in the following instances:

a. You attend a movie that has received good reviews. It has offensive language. You could...

_____

b. You are in a public crowd and hear someone curse or use crude speech. You could...

_____

c. A fellow Christian or spiritual leader speaks unkindly about a fellow member. You could...

_____

d. A family member curses at you in anger. You could...

_____

e. A rumor is going around your church about a member or leader. You could...

_____

f. A teacher makes a blatantly incorrect statement in class. You could....

_____

g. You are discussing a political matter with someone who disagrees with you. You could...

_____

The tongue can be both a dangerous weapon and a gentle blessing. It all depends on the words that come from it. God created our tongues to be good. Let us pray He helps us do so.

Heavenly Father, help me use my mouth to help people and give praise to Your name. Forgive me when I fail to do so. Amen

<u>One thing I learned from this session:</u>

"The Practical Disciple"
A Study of the Letter of St. James

Session 7
The Letter of James 3:13-18
+ + +

Wisdom from Above

*3 *[13]* Who is wise and understanding among you? By his good conduct let him show his works in the meekness of wisdom. *[14]* But if you have bitter jealousy and selfish ambition in your hearts, do not boast and be false to the truth. *[15]* This is not the wisdom that comes down from above, but is earthly, unspiritual, demonic. *[16]* For where jealousy and selfish ambition exist, there will be disorder and every vile practice. *[17]* But the wisdom from above is first pure, then peaceable, gentle, open to reason, full of mercy and good fruits, impartial and sincere. *[18]* And a harvest of righteousness is sown in peace by those who make peace.*

+ + +

The introduction to Session Six stated there are only two ways to live, either by the "wisdom" of the world, or by God's wisdom. Our modern world prides itself in knowledge which it often equates with wisdom. However, a person can be wise without necessarily be learned, and a learned person can be unwise. Knowledge is the sum of one's learning. Wisdom interprets and applies that knowledge in beneficial ways.

James 3:13-18 seems to echo Paul's assessment of the two kinds of wisdom in 1 Corinthians 1:18-25. Note any similarities with James.

1 Corinthians 1:18-25 (Paul)

18 For the word of the cross is folly to those who are perishing, but to us who are being saved it is the power of God. 19 For it is written, "I will destroy the wisdom of the wise, and the discernment of the discerning I will thwart." 20 Where is the one who is wise? Where is the scribe? Where is the debater of this age? Has not God made foolish the wisdom of the world? 21 For since, in the wisdom of God, the world did not know God through wisdom, it pleased God through the folly of what we preach to save those who believe. 22 For Jews demand signs and Greeks seek wisdom, 23 but we preach Christ crucified, a stumbling block to Jews and folly to Gentiles, 24 but to those who are called, both Jews and Greeks, Christ the power of God and the wisdom of God. 25 For the foolishness of God is wiser than men, and the weakness of God is stronger than men."

1. James' assessment of wisdom in 3:13-18 hinges on behavior. If a person wants to be wise, his actions must agree with his words. What does James urge that person to do in verse 13?

_____

2. What does *"meekness"* (James 3:13) have to do with wisdom?

_____

3. In verse 13, James speaks of jealousy and ambition among the wise. What does Paul say God will do to the worldly-wise person in 1 Corinthians 1:19?

_____

4. Which Old Testament verse is Paul quoting in verse 19? (Use your Bible to find this)

_____

5. Why is knowledge not the same as wisdom?

_____

6. What do you think James means (verse 14) about being *"false to the truth?"*

_____

7. If a person displays boasting, selfish ambition and jealousy (verse 14), what does verse 15 say about that person?

_____

8. James says an earthly wise person is *"unspiritual, demonic."* How is it possible a worldly-wise person could be considered demonic? In what way?

_____

9. In verse 16 James says, *"For where jealousy and selfish ambition exist, there will be disorder and every vile practice."* Could this also happen inside a church? Can you think of an example?

_____

10. Consider the most vile practice you've known of happening inside the Christian church. How could this take place?

_____

11. What do you think caused this practice?

_____

12. What could be done to correct it?

_____

13. Consider the most vile practice you've heard of happening in another religion. How could that take place?

_____

14. What do you think caused it and what can be done about it?

_____

15. Consider the problems the world has with radicalized Islam. How could jealousy and selfish ambition work together in the hearts of those who carry out their atrocities?

_____

16. What would James or Paul tell us to do about radical Islamists?

_____

17. After several verses of warning about the negatives that can arise from worldly wisdom and boasting, in verse 17 James goes to the positive. What eight things does he list will come when we follow the *"wisdom from above"?*

a. _____

b. _____

c. _____

d. _____

e. _____

f. _____

g. _____

h. _____

18. What do you think is meant in verse 18, *"a harvest of righteousness is sown in peace by those who make peace"?*

_____

19. What do you think Paul means in 1 Corinthians 1:18, *"But we preach Christ crucified, a <u>stumbling block</u> to Jews and folly to Gentiles."* Is Jesus also a stumbling block to Muslims?

_____

20. How would a crucified Jewish Rabbi be a stumbling block to the worldly-wise today?

_____

The Christian faith has a message to today's world, as it has had to every era: Trust in God, not in political power, or empty beliefs, or the human mind. There is more to life than this physical world, and more to life with God than rules. Forgiveness in Jesus is one thing dependable.

Heavenly Father, give us the grace to love those who hate us, and the courage to stand up in defense of the Gospel of Jesus Christ. Amen

<u>One thing I learned from this session:</u>

"The Practical Disciple"
A Study of the Letter of St. James

Session 8
The Letter of James 4:1-12
+ + +

Warning Against Worldliness

4 *¹ What causes quarrels and what causes fights among you? Is it not this, that your passions are at war within you? ² You desire and do not have, so you murder. You covet and cannot obtain, so you fight and quarrel. You do not have, because you do not ask. ³ You ask and do not receive, because you ask wrongly, to spend it on your passions. ⁴ You adulterous people! Do you not know that friendship with the world is enmity with God? Therefore whoever wishes to be a friend of the world makes himself an enemy of God. ⁵ Or do you suppose it is to no purpose that the Scripture says, "He yearns jealously over the spirit that he has made to dwell in us"? ⁶ But he gives more grace. Therefore it says, "God opposes the proud, but gives grace to the humble." ⁷ Submit yourselves therefore to God. Resist the devil, and he will flee from you. ⁸ Draw near to God, and he will draw near to you. Cleanse your hands, you sinners, and purify your hearts, you double-minded. ⁹ Be wretched and mourn and weep. Let your laughter be turned to mourning and your joy to gloom. ¹⁰ Humble yourselves before the Lord, and he will exalt you. ¹¹ Do not speak evil against one another, brothers. The one who speaks against a brother or judges his brother, speaks evil against the law and judges the law. But if you judge the law, you are not a doer of the law* *but a judge.* ¹² *There is only one lawgiver and judge, he who is able to save and to destroy. But who are you to judge your neighbor?*

+ + +

James continues his warnings that Christians must not live as the unbelieving world does. He uses the language of the Old Testament prophets, telling them that rejecting God's ways is spiritual adultery. It is seeking union with something other than the true God who loves us, which unfaithful people of past generations have done.

James urges them to return to the Lord in repentance. God is faithful, even when people are unfaithful. He has redeemed us by the blood of His Son Jesus, and He loves us, no matter what. God's love does not depend on our behavior, but on His promises to us in Christ Jesus.

1. What does verse 1 tell us is the cause of their quarrelling?

_____

2. Do you think they were actually murdering each other, as it seems to imply in verse 2? Have Christians done that in history?

_____

3. Give an example of murder due to desire.

_____

4. Define *"covet"* as mentioned in verse 2.

_____

5. What does *"you do not ask"* imply they should be doing?

_____

6. What do you think he means by, *"you ask wrongly"?*

_____

7. Prayer can be for several concerns: praise, confession, thanks, and requests. Which do we spend most of our prayers on? Why?

_____

8. In verse 4 James speaks in the manner of an Old Testament prophet. If God's people get too friendly with the world, what will surely happen?

_____

9. Can you give an example of what it means to be a *"friend of the world"* today?

_____

10. Where is the Bible passage quoted in verse 5?

_____

11. Where is the passage James quotes in verse 6? Why does James quote so much from the Old Testament?

Where_____

Why _____

12. What five things does James urge them to do in verses 7-8?

a. _____

b. _____

c. _____

d. _____

e. _____

13. What does James mean by *"double-minded"?*

_____

14. Why should they *"be wretched, weep, and mourn"?*

_____

15. Do you think James is telling them to turn their backs on the joys of the world? What do you think he means in verse 10?

_____

16. Does verse 11 apply only to believers? In what other instances might it also apply?

_____

17. What is your opinion about the language people use today when speaking about politics?

_____

18. Will passing laws about slander or offensive speech help make our public speech better? Why or why not?

_____

19. *"Speak evil"* in verse 11 denotes slander. What is "slander"?

_____

20. Verse 11 refers to God's Law. All of God's laws are to be obeyed. What are some of God's laws which people use to judge others today?

_____

21. Verse 12a warns us against judging God's laws. Why?

_____

22. Look again at verse 12b. Can you think of a famous Christian who recently said, *"Who am I to judge that behavior?"* Do you recall the circumstances?

_____

23. What is the difference between "judging" and "being judgmental"?

_____

Dear Jesus, help us watch our speech so that we may speak truthfully, yet in a spirit of love. Amen

One thing I learned from this session:

"The Practical Disciple"
A Study of the Letter of St. James

Session 9
The Letter of James 4:13-17

+ + +

Boasting About Tomorrow

4 *¹³ Come now, you who say, "Today or tomorrow we will go into such and such a town and spend a year there and trade and make a profit" — ¹⁴ yet you do not know what tomorrow will bring. What is your life? For you are a mist that appears for a little time and then vanishes. ¹⁵ Instead you ought to say, "If the Lord wills, we will live and do this or that." ¹⁶ As it is, you boast in your arrogance. All such boasting is evil. ¹⁷ So whoever knows the right thing to do and fails to do it, for him it is sin.*

+ + +

Like James' first readers, we strive to be self-sufficient and so we may develop detailed plans for our lives. Planning is always good stewardship so long as it does not crowd out the things God would have us do. James commands us always to seek what *"the Lord wills"* instead of relying on human cleverness alone.

Our lives are in God's hands. To seek God's will each day can show our dedication to Christian faith. It shows our faith and confidence in the Lord as we seek to live according to how He provides for us in our lives.

Time and again, God has shown His fatherly goodness and mercy toward us. He has given us earthly life for our days here in the world and eternal life in His presence through the sacrifice of His Son, our Lord Jesus Christ. Because we have our needs provided by Him, we now can serve others as we are able.

1. James now addresses those who believe they have done a good job of planning their lives. He warns them not to depend only on what they have done. Read and consider what Jesus says about this. What does He tell us in these verses from St. Matthew?

a. Matt. 6:19 _____

b. Matt. 6:20 _____

c. Matt. 6:21 _____

d. Matt. 6:24 _____

e. Matt. 6:25 _____

f. Matt. 6:33 _____

2. In light of these admonitions from Jesus, how can a Christian justify future financial planning?

_____

3. Check if any of the following apply to you.

_____ a. I've invested in the stock market or mutual funds.

_____ b. I've invested in a private business venture.

_____ c. I've lost money on some of my investments.

_____ d. My family and I have argued over investments.

____e. I wish I had made more investments earlier in life.

____f. I've made some foolish investments.

____g. I've worried too much about my investments.

____h. I have laid awake nights worrying about money.

4. What do you think is the difference between "proper" and "improper" plans a Christian can make for the future?

_____

5. Have you ever said to yourself, *"Today or tomorrow I will go into such and such a town and spend some time there and trade and make a profit"?* How did your plans turn out?

_____

6. James is not telling us it's wrong to plan for the future. But what is he telling us?

_____

7. Jesus advocated planning. How does He speak of it in Luke 14:28-30?

_____

8. Verse 14a is central to James' warning. What are those words?

_____

9. Verse 14b tells us a glaring truth — our life will not last forever. In fact, to what does James compare our life?

_____

10. How many of these documents do you have for your future?

____a. Last Will and Testament

____b. Life Insurance policy

____c. Advance Medical Directives (Living Will)

____d. Powers of Attorney for Financial or Medical matters

____e. Financial Trust for heirs

____f. Pre-paid funeral plan

____g. Purchased funeral plot

11. If you have most of #10 checked, congratulations. You're prepared to die! But what about the remaining days God will give you to live? Have you done anything to prepare for them?

_____

12. Many people have not only failed to make plans for their death, they don't even want to talk about it. Why might this be?

_____

13. What would you tell such a person?

_____

14. Verse 15 is central to James' directives. How are we to make our plans for the future?

_____

15. What does verse 16 say is the source of any boasting we may have over our self-accomplishments?

_____

16. Verse 17 tells us, *"whoever knows the right thing to do and fails to do it, for him it is sin."* Knowing what to do and failing to do it is sinning. What about the person who doesn't know what to do? If he fails to do it, is he still sinning?

_____

17. The Bible teaches that human beings are sinners from their very birth. We call this "Original Sin." The evidence of our "Original Sin" comes through "Actual Sins," those things we do (sins of commission) and those we fail to do (sins of omission).

Are there times when the church speaks too much about sin?

_____

18. Any of the sins of life are sufficient to condemn us in the eyes of Almighty God. However, God in His mercy sent His only Son Jesus to pay the penalty for our sins by dying on the cross. Any person of any age or ability, nationality or race, who trusts in

Jesus, however large or small their faith may be, will receive the gift of eternal life. For that we can never thank God enough.

Dear Lord Jesus, how can we ever thank You enough for Your mercy? Help us share Your love, that others may also believe and have eternal life. Amen

One thing I learned from this session:

"The Practical Disciple"

A Study of the Letter of St. James

Session 10
The Letter of James 5:1-6

+ + +

Warning to the Rich

5 *¹ Come now, you rich, weep and howl for the miseries that are coming upon you. ² Your riches have rotted and your garments are moth-eaten. ³ Your gold and silver have corroded, and their corrosion will be evidence against you and will eat your flesh like fire. You have laid up treasure in the last days. ⁴ Behold, the wages of the laborers who mowed your fields, which you kept back by fraud, are crying out against you, and the cries of the harvesters have reached the ears of the Lord of hosts. ⁵ You have lived on the earth in luxury and in self-indulgence. You have fattened your hearts in a day of slaughter. ⁶ You have condemned and murdered the righteous person. He does not resist you.*

+ + +

In this section, James condemns the wealthy for living for this life only, and as if Christ will not return. These are very "modern" thoughts, so a discussion of James' response is appropriate for Christians today.

God's Word repeatedly warns against unsettling attitudes which Satan uses to attack our faith. When we are young and "invincible," it's hard to be concerned about heaven. When we are older, we may wonder if heaven is real or just an idea dreamed up by others. Whatever temptations may come, it is important to trust God's promise that Christ will return in judgment.

It is also easy to think this passage only applies to the truly wealthy and greedy. But most of us are wealthier than 90% of the world's population. We must take care not to become disinterested or self-indulgent and waste the blessings God has given us.

Keep in mind Paul's words about genuine riches in 2 Corinthians 8:9, *"You know the grace of our Lord Jesus Christ, that though He was rich, yet for your sake He became poor, so that you by His poverty might become rich."* In Jesus Christ, we have the riches that come from God alone, those which come from the Holy Spirit's gift of faith.

1. One wonders what James is referring to here in verse 1. Did he know of the coming devastation of Jerusalem? Had he heard what Jesus said during His ministry about the day when *"not one stone will be left on another"* (Mark 13:2)? What other reason might James have in saying the rich will *"weep and howl"?*

_____

2. What is your definition of "rich"?

_____

3. Even the most wealthy must rely on God's providing their needs. What has been given liberally can be removed instantly. Read the story Jesus told in Luke 12:16-21.

    a. What moved the rich man to make his plans?

_____

    b. What were those plans and expectations?

_____

    c. What was the actual outcome?

_____

    d. What is the answer to God's question in verse 20?

_____

4. What happens to the rich man's old garments in James 5:2?

_____

5. Verse 3 speaks of gold and silver corroding. We hear today that precious metals are the only investment that *"will never be worth zero."* Do you think that's true? Why or why not?

_____

6. So what does James mean when he says their "gold and silver have corroded"?

_____

7. Our possessions are fleeting and will pass away. We work so hard for them, but they wear out, are used up or given to others. What do you think James means when he says their treasures *"will eat your flesh like fire"?*

_____

8. Verse 3 says, *"You have laid up treasure in the last days."* It almost sounds like a good retirement plan! What do you think of the American or world trend which spends so much effort on being prepared for retirement?

_____

9. In verse 4 James condemns the rich for cheating workers out of their wages. See Jesus' story in Matthew 20:1-16. We can assume the owner of the vineyard was wealthy. Was he trying to cheat his workers? What point was Jesus making?

_____

10. What does Jesus tell us about wealthy people in Matthew 19:23? Why are His words true?

_____

11. Read Matthew 19:20-22. What caused the rich young man's sadness?

_____

12. In today's world economy there are some incredibly wealthy people. A recent Chinese businessman sold his "Initial Purchase Offering" (IPO) shares for over $35 billion dollars. A story about his life said that less than twenty years before he had nothing but desire and an idea. What would you say to a fantastically wealthy person?

_____

13. What do you think would God say to such a person?

_____

14. What do you think wealthy people usually do with their wealth?

_____

15. If you were given one billion dollars, what is the first thing you would do with it?

_____

16. In verse 5, James condemns the wealthy who live in luxury and take advantage of the poor. What do you think he means when the Lord of Hosts says, *"You have fattened your hearts in a day of slaughter"?*

_____

17. What does greed lead to in verse 6?

_____

Wealth is a blessing from God. It is to be used to benefit others, not just be hoarded. If a person has been blessed with the ability to make money, he or she should make sure something good is done with it. We cannot demand the wealthy share their wealth. Neither should we call all wealthy person greedy. Each of us should be wealthy in sharing God's love with others, however we can do it.

Heavenly Father, help me not to put my trust in riches of this world, but in the riches of Your grace. Amen

One thing I learned from this session:

"The Practical Disciple"

A Study of the Letter of St. James

Session 11
The Letter of James 5:7-12

+ + +

Patience in Suffering

5 ⁷ *Be patient, therefore, brothers, until the coming of the Lord. See how the farmer waits for the precious fruit of the earth, being patient about it, until it receives the early and the late rains.* ⁸ *You also, be patient. Establish your hearts, for the coming of the Lord is at hand.* ⁹ *Do not grumble against one another, brothers, so that you may not be judged; behold, the Judge is standing at the door.* ¹⁰ *As an example of suffering and patience, brothers, take the prophets who spoke in the name of the Lord.* ¹¹ *Behold, we consider those blessed who remained steadfast. You have heard of the steadfastness of Job, and you have seen the purpose of the Lord, how the Lord is compassionate and merciful.* ¹² *But above all, my brothers, do not swear, either by heaven or by earth or by any other oath, but let your "yes" be yes and your "no" be no, so that you may not fall under condemnation.*

+ + +

As Christians, our knowledge and faith in the return of Jesus shape our life. Our confidence in His return should help us relate kindly to one another and caringly as we deal with sufferings in this life. God in His mercy promises to accompany us through our daily life and bring us to Himself at the end of time in eternal glory.

As weak human beings, we tend to focus on the small things of life and that everything depends on us. We think the quicker we can put a problem behind us, the better we will be. But this may not be God's perspective. He looks at the true goal, which is eternal life with Him.

Our sufferings may remain with us long term, but we can, with His strength, bear them with patience. God gives us faith to help us through our suffering, as well as confidence that we can endure all things until He comes again.

1. James tells us in verse 7 to be patient. What do you think can help us be patient until He comes again?

_____

2. James uses the farmer's patience as an example. You cannot hurry the seed's growth, for it has its own timetable. What will happen if we try to hurry the seed, or check continually to see how much it has grown?

_____

3. I once planted a garden and one day found part of a row of carrots had wilted. A careful check showed one of my little boys had pulled up some immature carrots to see how big they were. He replaced the dirt over them and thought they'd grow again. but they didn't. What lesson could be learned from this?

_____

4. Verse 7 speaks of the *"late and early rains."* The Israelite calendar called for its growing season during the months of February through May. With warmth and the early and late rains, the grain or garden would mature. If the farmer patiently awaits both, how does the Christian patiently wait?

_____

5. *"Establish your hearts"* (verse 8) is James' encouragement to be strong in the face of adversity. This life will not last forever, and the Lord will come soon. How can we await the Lord's coming?

_____

6. What do you think James means by *"the Judge is standing at the door"?*

_____

7. Of whom does James remind them if the people need patience in their suffering?

_____

8. If we ask Him, God will give us patience to remain steadfast until the coming of Jesus. Our faith will make us blessed. Who does James hold up as an example of patience in suffering?

_____

9. James here echoes the words his Lord Jesus spoke in Matthew 5:37. What can using oaths can lead to?

_____

10. If you are in a group, discuss Christian persecution as we see it today. Bring a newspaper article, or take notes of online information you can find of the terrible persecutions and deaths of Christians in the Middle East.

a. Why do you think this is happening so severely now?

_____

b. What world political factors that have led to it?

_____

c. What do you think our government should do about it?

_____

d. What can Christians be doing about it?

_____

e. What do you think such persecution means for us today?

_____

11. Discuss how verse 7 applies to facing persecution.

_____

Lord Jesus, protect Christians all over the earth from cruel persecution. Keep them faithful to You until Your coming in judgment. Amen

<u>One thing I learned from this session:</u>

"The Practical Disciple"
A Study of the Letter of St. James

Session 12
The Letter of James 5:13-20
+ + +

The Prayer of Faith

5 ¹³ Is anyone among you suffering? Let him pray. Is anyone cheerful? Let him sing praise. ¹⁴ Is anyone among you sick? Let him call for the elders of the church, and let them pray over him, anointing him with oil in the name of the Lord. ¹⁵ And the prayer of faith will save the one who is sick, and the Lord will raise him up. And if he has committed sins, he will be forgiven. ¹⁶ Therefore, confess your sins to one another and pray for one another, that you may be healed. The prayer of a righteous person has great power as it is working. ¹⁷ Elijah was a man with a nature like ours, and he prayed fervently that it might not rain, and for three years and six months it did not rain on the earth. ¹⁸ Then he prayed again, and heaven gave rain, and the earth bore its fruit. ¹⁹ My brothers, if anyone among you wanders from the truth and someone brings him back, ²⁰ let him know that whoever brings back a sinner from his wandering will save his soul from death and will cover a multitude of sins.

+ + +

In the manner of a prophet, James has been calling sinners to repentance. We must take care not to think our life is only between "God and me." We may try to hide behind our facades of obedience and perfection, but sin exposes us. It pervades every aspect of our lives. If left to ourselves, we could not live, and we would certainly not receive eternal life.

God has given us the Christian congregation, a body of people to help us in our spiritual journey. The members can teach us the Word, hear our confession, pray for our needs, praise the Lord with us in song, and bring us back when we wander from God's path. Most of all, they can remind us of the Gospel of Jesus and speak God's Word of His forgiveness.

1. In all circumstances, whether good or bad, what should Christians do for themselves and for others?

_____

2. How does the cheerful person assist others?

_____

3. Verse 14, James urges the Elders (congregational leaders) to pray for and anoint the sick. Anointing is a physical sign that can be done with prayer. In ancient times, what was oil used for?

_____

4. If it is done, what does James say should accompany it?

_____

5. Verse 15 says, *"The prayer of faith will save the one who is sick."* The Greek verb can also mean "will heal" the one who is sick, both healing of the body and of the soul through salvation. How important has prayer been in your life? Example?

_____

6. In verse 15 the words, *"raise him up"* is not about resurrection or "faith healing" but about making the sick person better through the prayers of others. What do you think of "faith healing"?

_____

7. Verse 16 urges us to confess our sins to one another. Have you ever experienced this? Did it help you?

_____

8. *"The prayer of a righteous person has great power"* is James' central thought in this passage. What person and circumstance does James point to as an example of powerful prayer?

_____

9. Where is the Old Testament passage found that explains the events in verse 17-18?

_____

10. What is James concerned about in verse 19?

_____

11. What might be an example of how we could *"wander from the truth"* (19)?

_____

12. How can we *"bring him back"?*

_____

13. What do you think is meant by *"save his soul from death"?*

_____

14. What will happen to a person left in sin?

_____

15. Read 1 Peter 4:8. What is it that covers our sins?

_____

16. The Letter of James stops abruptly. The "Practical Disciple" has said what he wanted to say. James may not have been one of the twelve original disciples, but he was an important person in the life of the early church, writing one of the earliest New Testament letters to Christians applying God's Word to their daily lives.

Thank You, O Holy Spirit, for giving us the Letter of James. Amen

One thing I learned from the Letter of James:

Robert L. Tasler

Rev. Robert L. Tasler is a native of Windom, Minnesota, and a career pastor in the Lutheran Church-Missouri Synod, a conservative Lutheran body in fellowship with dozens of similar churches around the world. A 1971 ordained graduate of Concordia Seminary, St. Louis, Missouri, Bob has served parishes in North Dakota, California, Utah and Colorado.

He and his wife Carol are retired and divide their time between Colorado and Arizona. They are parents of Brian, a Denver business executive in a non-profit organization, and Chuck and his wife Debbie, Christian Day School Teachers in Phoenix, as well as proud grandparents of three.

Author's other works are listed in the front of this book and can be found in detail at: http://www.bobtasler.com.

Printed in Great Britain
by Amazon

87217903R00047